MAXIMIZE
BUSINESS VALUE

Begin with the Exit in Mind

DAVID –
MAX the
VALVE !

TOM BRONSON

Tom Bronson
Published by: Business Mastery Publishing, a division of Mastery Partners, LLC
817.797.1488
www.MasteryPartners.com
www.TomBronsonSpeaks.com

Printed in the United States of America
First Printing 2019
First Edition 2019
ISBN : 978-1-7923-2875-6

10 9 8 7 6 5 4 3 2 1

Publishing Coaching by Rich Cavaness
Edited by Nancy Baldwin
Cover art and design by 99Designs

To my father, Bill Bronson.

You were my greatest mentor.

I miss you.

TABLE OF CONTENTS

Foreword

When Tom gave me the honor and asked me to write his foreword, I have to be honest, my first thought was to do what most people do who get asked to write forewords or provide a book testimonial. I'd say, "Sure Tom, I'd love to. You write it; send it to me, and I'll edit it and send it back!" In the meantime, I'd skim through the book, or not read it at all, and before you know it, with very little effort on my part, the foreword would be written, and the project completed.

I know how the process works, because when I wrote my book *ROE Powers ROI - The Ultimate WAY to Think and Communicate for Ridiculous Results,* I ran into the same situation. I resisted the urge then, too, and encouraged contributors to give me genuine feedback that I would publish as is, short of fixing grammar, of course. In return, I promised they would benefit more than I would receiving a testimonial for my book. My dad always told me to focus on the giving part, not the receiving part, and you will grow exponentially as a result.

After procrastinating for a few days, something dawned on me. I was being asked by an author and friend to write a foreword on a topic that I take very seriously in my business. The request came from a person I have not only engaged in the past, but who truly is an expert in preparing a business to run at its highest value in order to provide the stakeholders maximum return on equity. Isn't that the purpose of a business anyway? This request was also an opportunity to make time and work on my business and resist the constant gravitational force to be pulled into the business.

Selfishly speaking, I knew this exercise was an opportunity to put the day-to-day aside. It was an opportunity to make sure that myself and my leadership team were doing what is necessary to review and improve on the indicators that drive the business value of my fast-growing, digital marketing agency, Mojo Media Labs.

I initially fell into the trap of prioritizing other projects. I became complacent, allowing myself to be pulled into the day-to-day or work on activities that I just would rather work on. Mojo has won numerous awards recently, Best Places to Work in America, the coveted Inc 5000, American Marketing Associations Marketer of the Year, HubSpot's top level Diamond tier, and so on. We finished our best year ever then went on to complete our best first half ever. Why did I need to refocus on this now?

I have learned many things over the last twenty-two years of my life as an entrepreneur. I've seen thousands of business models as a sales and marketing agency, in addition to growing up in my parents' business. One lesson that stands out is to not let the highs get you too high and the lows get you too low. I imagine a bar that runs through this high and low wave. My objective is to slowly and consistently empower people to raise that business performance/value bar to add increasingly more business value without the emotions that come with the highs and lows.

Whether you are on a high or low right now, take time to look at your business value drivers and fix what you can. Stop doing, or improve on, what is not adding value, and identify new value drivers you can begin working on today. Some of the biggest value drivers we have built into Mojo are initiatives we started three to five years ago.

Just as with any book that is intended to add business value, it makes sense to revisit the material on a fairly consistent basis. I'm always surprised when I pick up on the small things that either I missed the first time around, or now see differently through the lens of new experiences, to drive improvement.

I did not always have the drive to add enterprise value. It's easier to work on what makes me comfortable or is more familiar. It's easier to keep peace with the team to lead work, than what I knew full well that was not adding the right value. It was easy to tell myself "I will get around to it," or "I'm busy, and I'll get to that later." It's easy to put this process in the important not urgent box, rather than in the urgent and important.

Then I realized it's much easier to maintain something than to build it in the first place. And the responsibility of maintenance does not always have to fall on my plate! It can be someone else's responsibility, but make no mistake, you should always be accountable for the results.

I am a big proponent of fully transparent open book management (OBM). This value driver not only allows us to track and improve on a weekly basis, but it empowers the entire team to take ownership. It empowers them to go beyond their predesigned responsibilities for their individual roles. They add value beyond themselves to build new value drivers or improve on the ones already in place. People will support what they help build.

What *Maximize Business Value* will do is allow you to take inventory of your current value drivers. It will give you and your team a constant feed of the right initiatives you can implement to raise your bar. If you have built the right culture, guess what? Your team wants to go above and beyond anyway. So, why not come out of the weeds or enter the uncomfortable zone? Nothing creative ever happens in a comfort zone. Why not provide a direction where you are getting weigh in from the people who lead various departments in the organization? Once you get buy-in, then ownership follows. With the right culture and a high level of commitment, then you can be running at peak performance—team engagement.

Tom's ten functional areas of business model came at the right time to help me identify areas of improvement. It will identify areas in your business, too, no matter what state you or your organization is in right now. I took Tom's five points of advice at the end of Chapter 5 to help me set proper expectations.

In the end, I reframed my picture of this task, from what could have been a distraction from my routine into reading this book and sharing my experience. It has really helped increase the value of my business management skills and my business. Thank you, Tom, as always, for pushing me to improve myself and my business.

Mike Rose

CEO, Mojo Media Labs

Author of *ROE Powers ROI -*

The Ultimate WAY to Communicate

for Ridiculous Results

INTRODUCTION

"The only reason to have a business is to sell it and get paid for it."
–Carl Allen
Entrepreneur, Investor and Dealmaker

There are countless reasons why business transitions fail. In fact, roughly 83 percent of businesses that go on the market don't sell.

That's worth repeating—83 percent of businesses that put themselves up for sale never close a transaction. That statistic means that a mere 17 percent exit successfully. And, family business transitions, or intergenerational transfers, are not much different. Only 30 percent of those businesses successfully transition to the next generation.

Let's examine why those precious few in the 17 percent minority succeed. A few of them are disruptive businesses that command a high valuation by large suitors. Some are just plain lucky —in the right business at the right time. But the majority of them have one thing in common. They are prepared.

Being prepared means that the business owner has defined an exit strategy and has relentlessly executed that strategy until he has reached his goal. He has focused on building long term value. Most owners have had great internal and external teams to help them achieve their final goal. And that goal has been to exit the business at the highest value possible.

Building value and transitioning a business is a process, and it takes time. It's a process very different from running a business on a day-to-day basis. Simply put, you just don't know what you don't know. But that's OK. This book will give you the information you need to start moving toward a successful exit.

TOM BRONSON

ACT ONE
THE CASE FOR EXIT STRATEGY

TOM BRONSON

CHAPTER 1
JUST THE FACTS

"Have you ever been driving down the highway at 75 MPH and you pass some idiot who is backing up on the shoulder because he missed his exit? That person is going to cause an accident, you think to yourself. Unfortunately, that's what most business exits look like!"
—Tom Bronson

Congratulations! You started or took over this business, perhaps from your parent or grandparent or previous owner, and built it to where it is today. No one on the planet knows how to run this business better than you. You have an amazing amount of tribal knowledge bouncing around in your head. You can solve complex problems on the fly. When it's time to sell, you'll just feel it in your gut, like most everything else in your business. So, you'll just call someone, list the business, sell it in a few months and roll on down the highway.

There are roughly twenty-eight million businesses in the United States. Of those, about six million have more than one employee, and the vast majority of those, 99.7 percent, have $100 million or less in annual revenue.

BUSINESSES IN THE US

	Revenue Range	Number of Firms (000)	Percent of Firms	Revenue (Trillions)	Percent of Revenue
Micro Market	Under $5M	5,678	93.9%	$3.57	12%
Lower Middle Market	$5M to $100M	351	5.8%	$5.84	20%
Upper Middle Market & Above	Over $100M	21	0.3%	$20.33	68%
Total Employer Firms		6,050		$29.74	
Non-Employer Firms		21,708		$0.99	
All US Firms		27,758		$30.73	

Corporate Value Metrics LLC 2013, Walking to Destiny, Christopher M. Snider 2016

Each year, approximately 250 thousand of these companies with less than $100 million in revenue will come up for sale, putting themselves on the market and looking for a buyer. Of those companies looking for a buyer, only 42,500 will actually complete a transaction.

ANNUAL ATTEMPTED TRANSACTIONS

Companies Under $100M Revenue	6,029,000	
Number Attempting Sale Each Year	250,000	4.1%

Of those that actually complete a transaction, nearly 60 percent of the sellers will be dissatisfied with the outcome, and 40 percent will be happy with the outcome a year after the sale.

OWNER SATISFACTION AFTER THE SALE

Dissatisfied Owners after 1 Year	25,500	60%
Satisfied Owners after 1 Year	17,000	40%

Digest that for a moment. Of all the businesses that come on the market, only 17 percent will succeed in closing a transaction. Fewer than one in five. A whopping 83 percent of attempted transactions fail.

TRANSACTION SUCCESS RATE

Process Terminated without a Transaction	207,500	83%
Process Ends with a Successful Transaction	42,500	17%

Sounds hard to believe, doesn't it? You work your butt off for fifteen, twenty-five, even fifty years with a goal of selling your business and traveling the world, retiring to your favorite vacation spot or volunteering more, only to find out that you are not able to sell the business into which you've poured your very existence. Or, you do get your life's work sold, but the selling price falls way short of your expectations. No one ever talked about that nightmare when you started your business.

Although there is a seemingly endless supply of articles written on wildly successful exits, with small companies gobbled up by giant behemoths for billions of dollars, the fact remains that these are the smallest minority of business transactions. Most sales are never written about, and certainly most failed exit attempts never make it into the press. So, we are left to draw conclusions based on the minority of transactions that do see the light of day.

Why do some business owners successfully exit, and others don't? Let's look at a common denominator.

CHAPTER 2
WHY BUSINESSES FAIL TO EXIT

"Failure is the opportunity to begin again, this time more intelligently."
–Henry Ford
Inventor, Businessman, Rejecter of Failure

Why do most businesses fail to exit? What you can you do now to get into the elite 17 percent club of owners who successfully transition out of their business?

There is very little good material on how to exit your business successfully. Having participated in one hundred transactions myself, I understand why most business sales wind up in that 83 percent category. It boils down to a lack of knowledge leading to little or no preparation.

Most entrepreneurs know how to run their business and how to do it successfully. Many times, that success drives a sense of invincibility and pride. Let's face it, that "I can do anything" attitude serves owners well as they build wildly successful businesses. When it's time to sell, they believe they'll knock it out of the park just like everything else, right?

Most entrepreneurs know tons about their business. In fact, it is likely that no one on the planet knows more about your business than you do. Unfortunately, unless you have been through a business transition before, you likely know very little about exit planning. And worse, there's darn few places to turn to get help or even know what to do next. So, when it's time to sell, where do you turn?

When you want to sell your house, you call a real estate agent, right? He will walk through the house, tell you what to do make it more salable, and then list the house on the multiple listing service (MLS), a universal database where you can find out everything there is to know about all the houses on the market. In business it's a little different. There is no MLS for businesses for sale. The capabilities of business sales experts range widely. If you're lucky enough to know someone who sells businesses, then you'll call that person when the time is right.

There are two general categories of professionals dedicated to selling businesses: business brokers and investment bankers. Business brokers typically work in the micro business category (less than $5 million in revenue), although some do broker larger deals. Investment bankers typically handle everything else. Most specialize in the middle market ($5 million to $1 billion depending on who you talk with). Most brokers and investments bankers have a particular industry on which they focus, although my experience has been that most will go anywhere.

So, you reach out to that acquaintance, and tell him it's time to sell your business. He jumps into action, slaps together a listing, and you're off to the races, right? Not so fast.

By the time you're ready to sell, it's too late to be proactive in preparing your business for sale. And yes, you need to prepare for sale, a process that can take several years under the best circumstances.

Brokers and investment bankers make their money at closing. It's a time-tested business model. They list your business either for free or for some reasonable retainer, and they make the bulk of their money when they help you successfully close a transaction. Therefore, it stands to reason that they need to close deals to make money, and so deal flow becomes very important to them. Rightfully, and in general terms, they are more concerned about closing a deal than improving the outcome.

Don't misinterpret what I'm saying. Brokers and bankers are not all focused exclusively on closing a deal. They are a necessary part of the deal ecosystem, and most exits involve one or the other. They are not all created equally, so it's important to find a good and reputable one when it's time to sell.

When you first bring a broker or banker in they can tell you a few things that will help your business show better, but they are typically not experts in dramatically improving the outcome. That process takes years, and they don't have that much time. Sure, they can recommend consultants who can help with dressing up the place and even slapping on a fresh coat of paint, but meaningful improvements that drive higher exit values just take time.

So, in the end, most exits fail because the owner does not start the process early enough to prepare the business for a successful exit. The simple answer is start early and have a strategic plan. A concrete exit plan provides the guard rails as you drive your business toward your ultimate goals and dreams.

Easier said than done.

CHAPTER 3
THE CASE FOR EXIT STRATEGY

"Always start at the end before you begin. Professional investors always have an exit strategy before they invest. Knowing your exit strategy is an important investment fundamental."
—Robert Kiyosaki
American Businessman and Author

As a business owner, you should always be thinking about your next move. The simple fact of the matter is that a solid plan to exit gives you some control over your small business's future. Think about it.

A solid exit strategy prevents most of the failed attempts to exit. But more than that, a well-designed exit strategy is just good business strategy. It is a guidepost for effective decision making in your business.

When faced with a strategic decision, if it does not increase the value of your business, you simply shouldn't do it. That does not mean that the additional value needs to be immediate. Some strategies take a seriously long time to realize value. But, if you can't articulate that value, don't do it.

According to The State of Owner Readiness™ survey first published by the Exit Planning Institute (EPI) in 2013 and updated regionally ever since, 74 percent of business owners have no exit plan. If you are like most business owners, and you don't have a strategy, a default strategy will ultimately become evident and probably not in a positive way. In fact, according to the EPI study, a full 50 percent of business transitions are not voluntary. One of my mentors used to tell me "If you don't have an exit strategy, then by default your strategy is to die behind your desk and leave the problem for your family and employees to deal with." Awesome.

Catastrophes Happen

While that result sounds harsh, it is the reality. We've all heard stories of businesses that are forced to liquidate or fire sale because of some disaster, probably one of the 5 D's (death, disability, divorce, distress or disagreement) or countless other risks that business owners don't like to think or talk about (see the chapter entitled Risky Business). Here are a couple of them I have witnessed firsthand:

The owner suddenly died and left the business to his spouse or children who have never worked in the business but need the cash out of it to live.

The largest customer suddenly gives notice and leaves for a competitor, and it was 50 percent of the business.

The market suddenly changed, and the company failed to adapt, so the sales are on a death spiral. The owner finally realizes that it's time to sell before it's too late. Guess what? It probably already is.

While these are nasty scenarios, they happen all too frequently. I'm betting that you've heard at least one story like this. Probably many more.

It's Personal

So, knowing that (1) we've all heard at least one story like this, and (2) the most common denominator for those few companies that actually exit successfully is having a solid plan to do so, why is it that 74 percent of business owners have no exit strategy at all? In talking with literally thousands of business owners, the reasons can be boiled down to three major things.

First, an exit is a once in a lifetime event. When it's time to exit, most business owners probably have never been through it before, so it becomes a classic "don't know what you don't know" scenario. Although they probably occasionally dream about some future exit, they just don't know where to start, and therefore fail to actually do so.

Second, the life of most owners is intertwined with the business. They can't fathom what they'll do when they are no longer working in the business. These owners haven't dedicated time to thinking about what they'll do in the "third act" of their lives, so they just delay the inevitable. They think to themselves "What the hell am I going to do after I sell this? Golf every day? I don't think so!"

Third, most business owners are afraid of that word EXIT! Why is it that business owners think that the word EXIT is a nasty little four-letter word? Let's explore a few possible reasons I've heard through the years (and that might be rolling around in your head).

Most business owners conjure up negative thoughts around the word "exit." To them, it brings images of abandoning the business and people that they have sometimes spent the better part of their lives building. They think about some uncaring, huge corporate entity taking over and destroying what they've meticulously built over many years.

Business owners think of losing the culture and the friendships. They think of losing a sense of purpose and reason to get up in the morning. They think about the customers and the employees who may get angry because they were sold out. They have heard horror stories of former business owners who regret selling their business.

A properly executed exit strategy actually helps prevent these catastrophes.

The term "exit" should be taken as action neutral. If it makes you feel better about the process, call it something else, like transition or transaction or succession. When I use those words in this book, you should take them as interchangeable.

CHAPTER 4
EXIT STRATEGY IS GOOD BUSINESS STRATEGY

"Our goals can only be reached through the vehicle of a plan.
There is no other route to success."

—Pablo Picasso

Artist and Innovator

The simple fact of the matter is that exit strategy is good business strategy. Yes, it's not easy. Few really good things are easy. But, the long-term benefits make it definitely worthwhile. Let me build the case.

Exit Planning Benefits

Exit planning can seem like a tedious process. Many people think that the reward for all that work comes way off in the future. Why in the world would a business owner want to put himself through that effort before it's really needed? Because, a well-designed exit strategy opens the doors to possibilities. In fact, a well-designed transition plan can deliver benefits in just a few short months. And, it provides options where none previously existed. It improves a business to the point that an owner might not want to exit.

Most business owners don't even realize what options they have for exit, but if they built a genuinely valuable enterprise, the options increase exponentially.

In fact, the most important outcome of good exit planning is that a business owner can define the process on his own terms. He can transition on his terms and not be a victim to the process defining him because some risk factor rears its ugly head. That's code for a lower valuation than he wants!

What makes a great and properly executed exit strategy? It has at least the following components. Some strategies have many more depending on size and complexity of the business.

The exit strategy—

- Identifies and removes risks, some of which may be in the owner's blind spot
- Increases the value of an enterprise
- Forces a business analysis
- Aligns people to function on the same page
- Provides contingency plans for unforeseen issues

- Helps an owner identify and tie together three of his biggest priorities: business goals, personal goals and financial goals (the three Ps). Those priorities surprisingly don't frequently align.
- Gives him options for a future transition that he may not even know about

Let's address each of these benefits briefly.

De-Risking

Just like any business owner, we all have blind spots. There are probably blind spots that, once we know about them are easy to solve. There are things like having shareholder and operating agreements and a solid buy-sell agreement if there are multiple shareholders. Many business owners realize they need those but think they will deal with them later and soon forget. Business insurance policies that were set up years prior, and automatically renewed without review, may need to be updated with things like business interruption, cyber security and key man insurance. These issues are all behind the scenes items, but we should also think about other risks in our business that might be easy to solve, like customer or supplier concentration risk and documented processes.

A great exit plan includes finding and addressing these risks in a business, ultimately leading to higher valuations. Look for more on de-risking in the chapter Risky Business, or go the Tools tab at www.MasteryPartners.com to download our free e-book, *The Blind Spot: Hidden Risks - What You Don't Know Can Hurt You.*

Creating Massive Value

Great exit strategies include building long-term and massive additional value in the business. Think about it. This strategy is the component that is missing from most exit strategies, because by the time you actually start taking action on selling, you're within a year or two of your exit event. That's just simply too late to increase the value of your business. Building massive value or increasing the value you already have in your business takes time.

Sophisticated buyers won't believe short term improvements in value. You'll need to have a solid track record, usually in the form of trailing twelve months (TTM), to demonstrate that what you've done is sustainable, and not some short-term blip on the radar. In most cases, it will take several quarters, perhaps even a few years, until all the things you've done to build massive value finally make their way to your financial statements and valuation.

Singing from the Same Songbook

Most business owners don't want their employees to know that they are thinking about selling the business. That's one of the strongest arguments for exit strategy being good business strategy. When you approach an exit as a business strategy to build value in the business, involving your team is as natural as involving them in their daily job functions. When you set out to improve long term value, you won't be shy about who knows, because a more valuable business is one in which most people want to work.

Later in this book, we'll talk extensively about how and when to involve your team. And, we'll make a strong argument to augment your internal team with an external team to help you build massive value.

Planning for the Unthinkable

No business owner likes to think about those things that will suddenly and dramatically change his business. We summarize them easily as the 5 D's: death, disability, divorce, distress and disagreement. Every business should have a plan for what happens in the case of death and disability of the business owner or other key people. Life happens. It is very possible that you or a key member of your staff will become disabled.

Distress comes in many forms, like a large customer serving notice that he is leaving you, or a key employee turning in two weeks' notice, or a breach of your systems exposing your customer's data. I could go on and on. And although never a pleasant topic, the divorce of a business owner or shareholder will likely trigger unintended consequences unless you're prepared for it. Finally, a great plan will also address what happens when a serious and irreconcilable disagreement arises between shareholders or other stakeholders.

All of these would impact a business to a far greater extent than most owners are prepared. An exit plan provides contingencies for these situations, reducing their negative consequences.

Identifying Priorities

In Exit Planning Institute CEO Chris Snider's book *Walking to Destiny*, the author talks about the three legs of the planning stool: business goals, personal goals and financial goals. Although in each of these priority items, the business owner is the common denominator, many times these three priorities are not aligned, causing tension and possibly friction.

Business owners should intentionally think through each of these different priorities and be prepared to articulate them, if for nothing else than to have peace of mind. However, the best exit and business strategies tie these three priorities together to form a unified set of goals and desired outcomes. When these three goals are working in concert, the business owner can increase velocity and drive massive value.

Providing Options on Exit

The Exit Planning Institute State of Owner Readiness™ survey, unveiled that two-thirds of all business owners don't know all of their options for transitioning their business and harvesting their wealth. Most owners think that an exit strategy is simply selling their business to an outside company, hopefully for a massive amount of money.

While that may be the ultimate result, there are other options that business owners should seriously consider. These options include intergenerational transfers, selling to business partners or management team, employee stock ownership plans (ESOP), outright sale to a strategic or financial buyer, or converting the business to a "mailbox" business. A mailbox business is one where the owner leaves the day-to-day operations but retains ownership and steps back as an owner rather than employee. A well-designed plan explores all of these options and helps an owner determine where he ultimately wants to land. Go the Downloads tab at www.MasteryPartners.com to download our free e-book, *Business Transition Options: Pros and Cons.*

Debunking the Assumptions about Exits

Now let's debunk some of the flawed thinking around exit strategies. Again, this is not an exhaustive list, just some of the high spots.

- I'm not ready now. My business will sell quickly. I'll call someone when I'm ready to sell.
- I already know what buyers want.
- I get calls from potential buyers all the time.
- I don't need a professional financial plan to know what I need to retire
- There's just too much to do to get this business where I want it to be. I'll start thinking about exiting in three to five years.

Now let's break these down.

I'm Not Ready Now

I'm not ready, or my business is just not ready now. But I'm confident it will sell quickly, so I'll call someone when I'm ready to sell.

The unspoken issue with this approach is that if you start to plan when you've decided it's time to exit the business, you have probably not prepared properly. Your odds of landing in the 83 percent that never close a transaction increase exponentially. At the very least, you'll likely be in the category of accepting an offer far less than you want or getting stuck with a deal that is less than desirable. If you start to prepare less than two years before the planned exit event, there is very little you can do to change the outcome. It is what it already is.

Truth be told, this approach is way more common than it should be. And, of course, the problem with this approach is that if you've never been through a transition event, you probably don't know what you don't know.

I recognize that some businesses have little time to prepare, usually for unforeseen circumstances. Frankly, if you have less than two years, you should focus on non-strategic issues and de-risking. While these activities typically add little short-term value, they are at least steps in the right direction and may help you position the business for a transition.

As far as selling quickly goes, there is precious little data on business transactions, but the average takes about a year. Some take much longer. Even if you have everything buttoned up perfectly, buyer due diligence can drag on for months prolonging the process and increasing the likelihood of the deal falling apart or the value lowering.

I Know What Buyers Want

Every buyer of every business has a different motivation. Some are looking for earnings, others are looking for recurring revenue, and still others are looking for market share or expanded markets. The truth is, no one really knows what a prospective buyer might be looking to purchase. Hopefully, if your exit process is designed well, you'll turn up prospective buyers you never even knew existed. Certainly, some exits are designed for one buyer, but most buyers are yet to be found.

Therefore, how can you know what a buyer wants before you know who the buyer might be? That's not to mean that you shouldn't have a good idea of what your buyers might be interested in. On the contrary, you should have clear targets in mind, but be open to the possibilities you can't imagine now.

The Buyers are Calling…

"People call me all the time." Here's a dirty little secret. They are calling everyone! They're prospecting! Let's just work the math.

If you're a lower middle market company, and for the sake of argument, let's call that what EPI calls it, $5 to $100 million annual revenue, then you are being stalked by every private equity (PE) firm on the planet. These PE firms have so much "dry powder" or committed capital that they have to invest. And, every one of them will tell you that they have been following your impressive story, and that they have serious interest in your market.

Let me be clear, this is not an indictment of PE firms. On the contrary, I think they play an essential role in the exit planning process. They are all just chasing the same targets.

According to Pitchbook, a leading research organization focused on alternative investment sources, there are about 3,500 PE firms globally. For the sake of argument, let's conservatively assume they have two or three analysts on staff. Think of these analysts as business development representatives. Most are required to make one hundred calls a day, but let's just say they actually make fifty. So, *3,500* firms *x 2.5* analysts *x 50* calls = *437,500* calls per day.

There are 6.03 million businesses with revenue under $100 million in America that employ people. Calling all of these businesses with the call volume listed above would take less than fourteen days. So, the law of averages tells us that you should get at least one call every fourteen days, just like everyone else.

Private Equity Firms	3,500
Average Number of Analysts	2.5
Daily Calls per Analyst	50
TOTAL CALLS PER DAY	437,500

US Companies under $100M	6,030,000
Number of Days to Call them all	13.8

And, by the way, your chances of being stalked by these buyers dramatically improve when you win awards or get on some published list. In my last business, we were on the Inc. 5000 list (fastest growing companies in the United States) four times, and the Fast Tech List (fastest growing tech companies in our region) six times. I was also a finalist for the EY Entrepreneur of the Year award, in addition to numerous other corporate and industry awards. Each time we "made the list," the phone rang off the hook. These callers had been following us for years and just wanted us to know that they are very interested in our space. Enough said. I'll let you draw your own conclusions.

I Don't Need a Financial Plan

Thinking you know how much you need to retire without having a fully baked financial plan is like driving at night with your headlights off. Not only can you not see the road, you also can't see your instrument panel. Do you know where you're going? How fast you're driving? How much gas you have? If you're even driving in the right direction? If you're going to hit a tree?

Look. In its simplest form, the purpose of having a professional financial plan is to know how much money you will need to live your lifestyle for the rest of your life. Certified financial planners take your entire financial picture into account, including what you spend to maintain your lifestyle. They simply run the math to tell you what you'll need to live that way for the rest of your life. Despite the fact that most of your net worth is probably tied up in your business, you need a financial plan. Add that to your To Do list. Then ask yourself, will your exit plan allow you to meet your lifestyle needs?

I Have Too Much to Prepare. Call me in Three Years

I talk to many owners who understand that there's just too much to do to get their business where they want it to be to exit. They believe they will spend time working on the right stuff and in three to five years, their business will be ready in that ideal state to sell. Of course, in reality, most business owners are lost in the day-to-day and won't spend time on planning for a future exit. Their business just commands too much of their time. So, erroneously, they think they will start thinking about exiting in three to five years. They say that for several years, so the three to five is an elusive target, ultimately a myth. (Just like the exercise program I plan to start every Monday) Commit to action now.

Closing Arguments

In this chapter, I've tried to build an argument for why exit strategy IS good business strategy. Here are the facts:

- Most companies don't sell. Even when they try to leave, most business owners are stuck with an illiquid asset, and their net worth cannot be monetized.
- Most successful exits are the result of advanced planning.
- Most business owners don't know the benefits of solid exit planning.

Chris Snider has about the best definition of exit planning I've ever heard.

"Exit Planning combines the plan, concept, effort and process into a clear, simple strategy to build a business that is transferable through strong human, structural, customer and social capital. The future of you, your family, and your business are addressed by exit planning through creative value today."

Through solid exit planning, you can—

- Build, harvest and preserve wealth
- Identify, protect, build, harvest, and manage enterprise value (EV)
- Simplify the exit process and clarify the roadmap to success
- Integrate your personal, financial, and business priorities into one master plan

You have read this far and no longer have that excuse. If you still don't think you need an exit strategy then set this book aside, but keep it. Someday, you will need it, and you'll thank me.

If you want to take action now to secure the best possible outcome when it comes time to exit your business, then turn the page and keep reading.

I rest my case.

Chapter 5
Maximize Your Asset!

"Take this job and shove it!"

—Johnny Paycheck

Country Music Singer, Songwriter, Outlaw and Philosopher

One step in the right direction to a successful exit is to think of your business as an asset. It's not your child or your baby. It's an asset. And, just like any other asset, it has (or should have) value.

Every business has a backstory. Some of them are downright riveting. Others are, dare I say, ordinary. Regardless of the details of your backstory, if you were the original founder of the company, it probably goes something like this—

You found yourself out of work, either voluntarily or involuntarily.

You saw a need for some product or service.

You got very excited about creating something new, so much so that you poured your entire life savings into it.

You launched your company with visions of a great future.

You dreamed that someday you would sell your business and retire in style.

Then, somewhere along the way, the business became successful, and then something unexpected happened.

You got caught up in the daily grind, and the business turned into a source of income and lifestyle. It became a job, and you stopped thinking about the business as an asset.

Sometimes this cycle takes years. Sometimes it happens so quickly that you didn't really have the time to suffer. If the latter describes you, you're lucky! For most of us, the struggle was real. The pressure was enormous. The risk was more than just money. It was spouse and family. It was future security. It was life on the edge.

But, now you've made it through the eye of the needle, it's time to enjoy the spoils. After all, the spoils are what made the struggle worthwhile, right?

Don't get me wrong. I'm not saying that you shouldn't eat what you've killed. Quite the opposite. I'm suggesting that you can enjoy the spoils AND continue to think about your business as an asset. And, if you do that relentlessly, the spoils will be greater than you can imagine today.

You see, you just think differently about a job than you think about an asset. A job is a source of income.

A job provides for your family, and a job is usually easily replaceable.

An asset is precious. An asset is something for which you've worked hard. An asset has emotional ties for you and for your family. An asset has value. An asset is something that you can extract money from in the future. If you're fortunate enough to have children, I'm guessing you don't think about them as an asset. Why then, would you consider your business to be your baby?

In fact, many owners leave a tremendous amount of value on the table when it's time to exit. They are focused on income generation (a job), rather than being focused on building enterprise value (an asset).

When your primary objective is to improve long-term value rather than short-term profit, you invest differently. And make no mistake, every dollar you put into your business, whether it's out of your pocket or reinvested profit, is an investment. You should never spend money on anything in your business. It should never be just an expense. You should always think of money spent in your business as an investment. You shouldn't invest a single dollar unless you can clearly articulate the return on investment (ROI).

In my last company, every time one of my managers or front-line employees asked for money to invest in systems or software or whatever, they already knew I was going to ask, "What's the ROI?" And if they couldn't clearly articulate it, they wouldn't get the money. In fact, it became such a mantra for me that the long running joke around the office was "Tom wouldn't invest in toilet paper unless he understood the ROI!" Thank goodness I did!

So, how can you have your cake and eat it too? How can you enjoy income and lifestyle AND build value in this asset that someday you'll be able to monetize? The process starts by trying to balance conflicting priorities with the end in mind.

You have constant internal conflict of competing priorities. You are fighting a battle every day. That battle is between the owner and the employee. I'm not talking about between you and your employees. You are on both sides of this battle. On the one hand, you're the employee, or operator, who deserves a high income and the perks that come along with delivering results. On the other hand, you're the owner who demands those results and more, because you're trying to build long term value.

Owners and operators think at different levels. There is no better or worse. No right or wrong. Just a different approach. Most business owners are operators who get the job done and deliver the results. Far fewer act like owners.

If you want to eat your cake and have it too (which is the correct use of that phrase), you need to learn to be both. It is a delicate balance.

The employee just wants to get the job done. The owner wants the job done right. The employee wants to know why he can't put more resources into a project. The owner wants to drive efficiency. The employee wants benefits like vacations where he can get away from work for a while. The owner keeps the cell phone turned on in case of an emergency. The employee wants to be paid well now for his hard work. The owner knows that there is a bigger payday in the future. The size and terms of that payday are dependent on building value in the business today.

Decide that building long-term value in this asset is the most important outcome. Maximizing that asset, and valuing your business correctly, is a step in the right direction. You need to decide to quit your job today, and start acting like an owner.

CHAPTER 6
AVOID VAGUE VALUATIONS

"The only valid and accurate method for valuing a small business is to find a willing buyer and a willing seller who agree on price."

—Tom Bronson

Identifying value is a central part of exit planning. One of the reasons that 83 percent of exit strategies fail is that owners have an unrealistic expectation of the true value of their business. Over the years, I've come to realize that this error is caused by a number of factors.

Unicorn Valuations

First and foremost, there is precious little data regarding transaction statistics, particularly as it relates to non-publicly traded companies. The only real news that people can find on a regular basis is from large publicly traded company acquisitions, or some disruptive technology company sale, or investments made in "unicorns." A unicorn, of course, is what the investment world calls a private company, typically a startup, that has a valuation north of a billion dollars.

I won't get into my opinions regarding unicorns. Purely based on my definition above, these unicorns are able to attract investors at their valuation so it would appear that the valuation is valid—at least to the people writing those checks. Those valuations are wildly inflated compared to any other reasonable valuation method. Therefore, due to the publicity surrounding them, people are left to draw their own conclusions about this valuation being the norm.

Of course, if a company has some wildly disruptive technology or business model—think of companies like AirBNB, Uber or Tesla—no rules regarding valuations really apply. Again, because of the massive press around these types of companies, the average person is driven to think that these valuations are the norm for all businesses, rather than the exception.

The Retirement Requirement

One of my favorite valuation methods is the "what I need to retire" method. Don't laugh. I did the first time I heard this requirement years ago, but it's really more common than you think.

Several years ago, I was leading a massive rollup in the retail technology space. My team was buying companies at a pretty healthy clip. We used a clearly defined, proprietary valuation method that made it very easy for us to make an offer and cut right to the chase regarding whether a seller was serious or not. We typically wound up purchasing about one in ten of the companies with which we talked. For most companies, we never got to an initial offer, but for those we did, it certainly led to some interesting conversations. One in particular stands out.

We were looking at a software company that would have been a great tuck-in. These transactions are also called a bolt-on, which is an acquisition that adds value and can be rolled into an existing business. It had about $900 thousand in revenue and had been losing money for several years. Based on our valuation model, we could get to somewhere between $750 thousand and $1 million for our initial offer, not bad for a company that had been bleeding red ink for a long time.

When I tossed that offer to the owner, his response was that the company was worth about $4 million. At this point I started probing about how he came up with that valuation hoping that we could find some common ground, and his response was classic. "Well, that's what I need to retire."

On the inside, I was screaming "REALLY? That's your valuation method?" But what I said was "Well, most buyers are not particularly altruistic in their valuation methods, but if that's what you need, if you'll give me another thirty minutes, I'll tell you how to get there. And if you follow my advice, you'll be worth that much in two or three years, and I'd be happy to pay that price, or even more, if you achieve the results."

I then proceeded to outline the changes that needed to be made in his business, and before we hung up, we agreed that he would reach out in a year with a progress report. So, what happened when he called? Sorry, that's a trick question. Of course, he didn't call. He was too busy living his lifestyle business to make the necessary improvements to get his valuation. Last I heard, his revenue had dwindled even further, and the company may have ultimately folded. It's a shame, really. I was hoping he'd turn it around and sell it to me.

The X Factor

Another fun and common valuation method I hear on a regular basis is the "We've invested X dollars, and so we need at least that to sell the business." Now, if you're genuinely a unicorn with some disruptive technology, that requirement might be a valid valuation method. Then again, if you genuinely have disruptive technology, you're probably not looking to sell the business for merely what you've invested.

Several years ago, I had a conversation with a company looking to sell because their shareholders had investment fatigue, a frequent outcome when companies fail to achieve projected results and early investors want out. In reviewing the financial performance of the company, I learned that they had invested capital of nearly $10 million but had only delivered a few hundred thousand in annual revenue.

The company had existed for a number of years, and the owners poured their investment into product development. Granted the product was pretty slick, but it was by no means disruptive. It was an "also ran" in a particularly crowded space. Had they delivered the product soon after they started, they had a chance to be a leader. But it took so long to develop that there were already too many entrenched products on the market, and their relevance was waning.

In talking with the company, I told them the painfully obvious. "It's just not worth what your investors have put into the business, so either they need to be willing to take a huge loss or make additional investments to get the sales engine off the ground." That launched into what I lovingly call the Shark Tank conversation. You know the one from the popular television show. A person comes in to pitch a startup, has a wildly inflated and unsubstantiated valuation, and Mr. Wonderful, Kevin O'Leary, pounces. I love that part. Many times, I find myself laughing at his methods, but his message is usually spot on.

Country Club Valuations

Finally, there is the phenomenon of the Country Club valuation. This is the one that's really hard to overcome. It starts when your buddy at the club sells his business and the buzz starts about how much he got for his business. "I heard he got $10 million. I know my business is worth more than that, so my asking price is at least $10 million."

There is so much wrong with that valuation, I don't even know where to begin. Was your buddy in the same business? What was his revenue and EBITDA compared to yours? Was his business in a hot market? How did his company's operations compare to yours? What about his preparedness to sell his business?

I could go on and on and on. Typically, and interestingly, there is probably no basis for the rumored $10 million sales price. Your buddy probably never actually told anyone what he got for his business, but when someone tossed out the $10 million figure, he just sheepishly grinned, and the rest is history.

The news spread like wildfire in the club, and the fish tale got bigger every time. It's sort of like the telephone game we all played as kids when you sit in a circle and the first person whispers something to the person on his right, who whispers it to the next person and so on until it gets back to the original person. By that time, the message has changed so dramatically that it's usually unrecognizable. Don't be fooled by country club valuations. They are rarely based on fact.

Professional Estimates

The best solution is to prepare your business for sale by planning ahead. Get a regular estimate of value from a professional who does that for a living. Really good investment bankers and business brokers will usually provide this estimate at a minimal cost or in some cases free of charge. They are going to take all of the right factors into consideration and compare it to data that is not readily available on the open market.

Certified Exit Planning Advisors (CEPA) provide this analysis as a matter of course. More detailed valuations are available from valuation experts at a price. For the typical purpose of planning, an estimate or opinion of enterprise value is a great place to start. With this estimate in hand, you can develop a long-term strategy for the future.

If you'd like a free list of things you can do right now to improve value, go the Downloads tab at:

www.MasteryPartners.com to download our free e-book, *Things You Need to Think About to Improve the Value of Your Business.*

ACT TWO
LET'S DO THIS

TOM BRONSON

CHAPTER 7
START HERE

"To begin with the end in mind means to start with a clear understanding of your destination. It means to know where you're going so that you better understand where you are now and so that the steps you take are always in the right direction."

–Stephen Covey

Author and Educator

According to data collected by The Value Builder System from over 50 thousand business owners, the number one reason preventing owners from selling their businesses is fear of not getting what their business is worth. In fact, over 60 percent say that reason is what's preventing them from formulating an exit strategy. There is one way for them to guarantee they won't get what they think it's worth—not plan for it.

It's time for that thinking to stop. Getting the valuation an owner wants and needs requires advance planning. It's time to start thinking about that future event. Now that you are, where do you start?

Prolific writer and sales guru Jeff Gitomer said it best. "You already know what's wrong, so why don't you kick your own ass?"

I can't tell you how many times I've talked with a business owner who says his company is in great shape, and he gets calls from buyers all the time. Hmmm. Every company gets fishing calls from potential buyers. This could be part of the reason that owner expectations are so far out of whack. Most of these calls are from entry level folks who are dialing for dollars.

I recently talked with a business broker who told me he makes 500 calls a day looking for companies to sell. As I've mentioned before, most of these calls are not targeting you specifically. Instead, they are just looking for a business, any business, to sell. That's not to mean that there aren't targeted calls, because I've been on the receiving end of many. Those callers already know about that business. They are specifically looking to make an investment in that industry, or already have a business they are looking to grow inorganically through acquisitions.

When you get those calls, it creates a sense of complacency. You start to think that you can get your price because there are so many interested parties. And, if you are sincerely ready to sell, meaning that you've thoroughly prepared your business for a transition, you might be right. But, if you're the vast majority of all businesses out there, you are nowhere near ready, and you're only setting yourself up for disappointment. You may be working with a vague valuation.

While you're fielding those calls, doesn't it make sense to also start preparing your business for sale? If you're like most business owners, you have no idea where to start, so let me outline a plan that will at least get you moving in the right direction.

Connect with a CEPA

A Certified Exit Planning Advisor (CEPA) is a great place to start. CEPA is a certification offered by the Exit Planning Institute where candidates undergo rigorous training to learn how to help business owners navigate the exit planning waters. After hundreds of hours of training, CEPAs sit for a certification exam, just like other trained professionals.

Some CEPAs are attorneys or estate planners or financial professionals. Some have other professional designations, like CPA or CFP. Still others are value builders trained in helping businesses increase long term value. You can learn more about CEPAs and the Exit Planning Institute at their website, www.exit-planning-institute.org.

A CEPA can help you get your business in order. However, if you'd like to do some of it yourself, here's how to get started on your own.

Look for Low Hanging Fruit

Figure out what the low hanging fruit is, and knock it out. Start with the easy stuff in your business. Get your corporate records in order. Make sure that you've settled and documented all of your outstanding shareholder issues. If you're the sole shareholder, it's easier, but you probably still have some work to do. If you have more than one shareholder or if you have partners, make sure that you have all of the right agreements in place. You should have a shareholder agreement, or partnership agreement, and make sure you have a buy-sell agreement to resolve contingent issues.

Take Time to De-Risk

Have answers and contingency plans for the Five D's: death, divorce, disability, disagreement, and distress. Think about what will happen if one of these Five Ds rears its ugly head. Have a written plan, mostly in the form of an agreement, in place to handle it. What happens if you, or one of your partners or shareholders dies, becomes disabled and can't work, or gets a divorce? What happens if you get into disagreements with your shareholders or partners? What happens if one of your shareholders or partners or key employees suddenly leaves the business? These issues are not always easy things to resolve, but they are a great place to start. Think of this exercise as "de-risking" the business.

Plan Act Three

Think about what happens next. You will need to really spend some time thinking about your own future. When do you want to exit the business? What will you do when you exit the business? Are you sure what you're planning will be as fulfilling as running the business? For more on this topic, see the chapter entitled "The Third Act."

Examine Personal Finances

Get your personal financial house in order. Even though probably over 80 percent of your net worth is tied up in your business, you need to have a financial professional work up a real financial plan. These professionals include a certified financial planner (CFP) and preferably also a CEPA. Just because you think you need $3 million to retire does not mean that's the right answer.

Get professional help to make sure you'll have enough to do what you really want to do after you sell the business. Professionals also will help you evaluate the business in regard to a future sale. A good evaluation will include an assessment of your readiness as well as some sort of valuation.

Consider the Mastery Partners Way

At Mastery Partners (MP), our motto is "Transition on your Terms," and it is our mission to change the outcome for our clients by helping them identify, protect, build, harvest, and manage business value. We are also passionate about making sure our clients can successfully carry out their transition strategy, regardless of what it looks like.

Initially, we take a two-step approach. First, we perform a Transaction Readiness Assessment, called a TRA. The primary objective of this first step is to evaluate the business regarding its current state to identify possible areas that need attention in order to build long term value and prepare for a future transition event.

Just like author Stephen Covey says, "... You better understand where you are now... so that the steps you take are always in the right direction."

The Mastery Partners signature TRA is a tool designed to score your business across a variety of functional areas regarding the current state of readiness, as if a transition were to happen tomorrow.

Don't be fooled by the word "transaction" in the name TRA, though. The majority of our clients are not really looking to sell their business any time soon. In fact, most of the MP clients have a three- to five-year transition horizon, and some much longer. Frankly, our business is to help you improve the EV, the total value your business is worth, and that takes time. Additionally, many MP clients have no plans to sell their business at all, but want to have more options when the time is right.

Mastery Partners typically only works with clients who have at least three years to prepare for some exit event, because there is little we can do to help a business that is urgent to sell in less than 18 months. In that short time frame, all we can do is slap on a fresh coat of paint and present your business in the best possible light in its current state. That solution goes against our core mission to improve the ultimate outcome for our clients.

The functional areas we typically evaluate in most businesses include—

- Corporate Governance: Are your records and affairs in order?
- Legal Matters: Are there any current or potential legal threats to your business?
- Finance and Accounting: Is your financial house in order?
- Human Resources: Are you protecting your most valuable assets?
- Operations: Do you have easy to follow and documented processes in place?

- Sales & Marketing: Are you growing and does your business have a positive outlook?
- Strategic Planning: Have you planned for the future as if you're going to own the business for twenty years?
- Succession Planning: Are the right people on the bus, and do you have contingency plans?
- Product and Development: Is your product and strategy forward thinking enough?
- Infrastructure and IT: Can your infrastructure support the future?
- The deliverables for the transaction readiness assessment are—
- A Heatmap, which is a comprehensive report based on many hours of research. It includes investigation and confidential interviews with relevant parties, typically the owners or in larger businesses the management team, that will highlight the opportunities in your business. The heatmap will identify improvements that will ultimately impact the enterprise value of your business, whether you choose to sell it or not.
- An Opinion of Enterprise Value of your business based on current trends, available industry data, financial performance and more. It is important to note that this result is only an opinion. The fact

of the matter is that there is only one way to truly value a small to midsize business (SMB) and that is to have a willing buyer and a willing seller who agree on price.

Once the TRA is complete, a review meeting is held to go over the findings and the valuation opinion. At that point, our clients have the option to use the information to make improvements on their own, or move to the second step in our process, the Roadmap for Value Acceleration (RVA).

With the RVA, we take the data from the TRA and assemble a strategic action plan. The goal of this roadmap is to achieve sustainable results in key operating areas to build long-term value for a high-yield event. Think of it as a business plan on steroids. The roadmap also addresses other strategic opportunities uncovered during the TRA. It will assemble a work plan to make improvements, along with dependencies of each action step, so you can see the proper order to take action.

Once we complete the roadmap, our clients again have the option to take a do-it-yourself approach, or partner with Mastery Partners to assist in the implementation.

Note that we say assist, because preparing your business for sale will require work on your part, and that of the talent in your organization, to implement the recommendations. You can't just outsource the whole thing. Anyone who says you can is leading you down a slippery slope. Our RVA includes a proposed strategy and timeline to implement. Regardless of whether our clients engage with Mastery Partners or take the DIY approach, MP maintains routine check-ins at a cadence appropriate to the project. These check-ins ensure that the implementation is progressing according to plan.

A free e-book about the Mastery Partners Process - *The Mastery Partners Way* - is available to download at www.MasteryPartners.com.

This approach is what a good process looks like. It is what I have used time and time again to achieve successful exits. Now, I share all this with you not as a hard sell that you should engage with Mastery Partners, but more as an overview of a good strategy. If you have a CEPA you're working with, the process will look very similar to what I've outlined above.

My final advice:

- Start early.
- Don't wait until you're ready to sell the business. You should start a process at least three to five years before your ideal exit time. Even if you haven't determined when you'd like to exit, it's never too early to start the process.

- Be flexible once you start marketing the business.
- In one of my recent transactions, the buyer was originally scheduled to close the deal in September, which slid to November, which slid to December, and ultimately closed on the last day in February. John Warrilow said it best "Rigid sellers don't sell."
- Plan for your future.
- It should include a happy, lucrative exit and a plan for what you'll do next in Act Three.
- Be ready to articulate your expectations and desires to your family, your partners and your staff. Of course, you can't do that until you've actually thought it through in advance!
- Although it's sometimes hard for a successful business owner to do this, make sure to check the ego and emotion at the door before you start.
- A good intermediary, business broker, or investment banker can be a good partner to help you do that.

Planning ahead not only provides an opportunity to avoid disaster and maximize profits, it opens the door to strategic options.

TOM BRONSON

CHAPTER 8
CONSIDER ALL OPTIONS

"Having only one option is not an option."

—Unknown

The Exit Planning Institute takes a periodic poll of business owners called the EPI State of Owner Readiness Survey. In the most recent survey, two thirds of all respondents were not aware of all of their exit options. Only three out of ten business owners knew the options to successfully exit their business.

Part of the reason is because owners don't like to talk about exit strategies. Therefore, when a knowledgeable person starts talking about options for exit, the owners turn and run the other direction as fast as possible.

To make the discussion easier, this chapter offers a quick overview of the various options available to transition out of a business. In broad strokes, the options to sell a business fall into these categories:

- Internal Transition: Transitioning your business to someone currently in the family or business

- External Transition: Selling your business outright to a third-party buyer or an initial public offering (IPO)
- Role Transition: Remaining the owner but transitioning out of the day-to-day operations of your business
- Liquidation: Selling the business assets through an orderly liquidation process.

Internal Transitions

Perhaps you want to transfer your business to someone on the inside or a family member. This approach is called an internal transition. The options for this type of exit strategy include transitioning the business to the next generation, selling it to your employees through a management buyout (MBO), or selling it to your employees through an Employee Stock Ownership Plan (ESOP).

It's important to note that an internal transition typically nets a lower valuation. You are selling the business in a friendly transition to family or insiders who probably already know a great deal about the business. However, make no mistake, this type of transition needs to be handled as professionally as any other type of transition where agreements are documented and memorialized.

External Transitions

If you've decided the right move for you is to sell the business to a third party, that is called an external transition. A transaction of this type can include an outright sale, a recapitalization or even an IPO. For the purposes of this book, we will not address IPOs, but know that if an IPO is your ultimate goal, good luck, and there is an endless supply of good information available to you. I almost went down that path in the mid 90s. Thank goodness a publicly traded company came along and took pity on this poor, defenseless creature and saved me from the pain and anguish of going through an IPO. If that's your path, then heaven help you.

IPOs aside, the most common transition is external, identifying and attracting an outside buyer for your business. Some sellers determine to go it alone down this path. There is some, albeit very little, success in a self-directed sale, particularly if the seller has little to no experience in selling a business.

Most sellers, however, decide to get professional help to sell a business, choosing either a business broker or investment banker, depending on their size. As a former investor once told me "In business, size matters." Typically, businesses under $5 million in revenue (micro businesses) use business brokers, and businesses over $5 million in annual revenue use investment bankers, although many investment bankers don't serve clients under $50 million.

Role Transition

Many of our clients tell us that they don't want to sell their business at all. Rather, they want to convert it into a "mailbox" or "sailboat" business. These are terms for absentee owners who live on a sailboat or stop into the post office monthly to collect and deposit their checks from the business(es) they own. In this type of transition, it's imperative that an owner document his processes and procedures to ensure that he can hire management to run the company while he pursues more amusing activities.

As the baby boomer generation is aging, role transitions are becoming more common, because baby boomers just don't want to completely retire. After all, the baby boomer generation invented the sixty-hour work week. In order to effectively transition to a mailbox business, rather than owner/operator, an owner will have to learn to let go of the day-to-day. But, if he can master that, it is a great way to transition and reap the rewards without actually selling the business.

Liquidation

Finally, no list of transition strategies is complete without a mention of liquidation. While liquidation conjures up sad thoughts about businesses that are forced to close and sell their assets, it is a legitimate transition strategy and has a time and place. The best liquidation, of course, is the orderly liquidation where an owner sells the assets as quickly as possible to monetize the value.

I recently advised a client that his best transition might be an orderly liquidation. Based on his valuation and desired outcome, a liquidation was the best alternative to quickly monetize his value and transition his business. In this case, the liquidation value far exceeded the fair market value of his business. Therefore, liquidation was a good alternative for him, especially considering that he had not prepared his business in advance for transition.

The Final Analysis

By preparing before it's time to execute, you'll have so many more options available to you when the time is right. And you'll be better able to plan for the future.

Download the free *Business Transition Options* e-book from the Downloads tab at www.MasteryPartners.com.

TOM BRONSON

CHAPTER 9
PLAN FOR SUCCESS

"If you fail to plan, you are planning to fail."
—Probably not who you think

"Why couldn't X company find a buyer?" I get asked this question frequently. Sometimes, as I am presenting to a larger audience, and I tell them the astounding stat of 83 percent of companies that list never close a transaction, their reactions are gasps and disbelief. My answer is the same for all of them. Business owners fail to plan for a successful exit from their business.

But why? Planning for success seems like a critical responsibility of owning a business.

Business owners are so caught up in the day-to-day operation of their business, that selling it or retiring from it, or transitioning it to the next generation is something they think about later. They say, "There's too many things going on now to think about exit strategies. Take time to plan now? Are you kidding? There's so much to do!" or "I don't have time," or "There won't be a business to sell if I don't get this done." And in the same breath they say, "I'm going to sell this company in three to five years," something the average business owner says for nearly twenty years before he takes action.

Benjamin Franklin is often credited with the adage "By failing to prepare, you are preparing to fail," or something like that. However, most scholars would agree that this popular saying is most likely incorrectly attributed to Franklin, who was first credited with it in a 1970 newspaper filler. You can find similar sayings in many places in literature. Perhaps my favorite is from Robert Schuller's book *You Can Become the Person You Want To Be,*

"Remember: Most people fail, not because they lack talent, money, or opportunity; they fail because they never really planned to succeed. Plan your future because you have to live there!"

This remark perfectly captures my sentiment. People don't fail to plan for their exit strategy because they lack talent or opportunity. In fact, by definition, most entrepreneurs are risk takers. They started their business because they found some need for a product or service, and they probably risked everything to start their business. These business owners are probably the most talented people in their fields, so the fact that they don't plan for their exit is not a result of their lack of intelligence.

In my initial meetings with prospective clients, I typically hear some form of the following statements in response to my questions about exit planning:

- I haven't really done any planning, because I just don't know what questions to ask.
- I don't even know where to start.
- Nearly 100 percent of my net worth is tied up in this business. I really didn't think it was appropriate to plan, because I don't know what it's worth.
- I don't know my options.
- I'm not really ready to sell now. I'll think about that in five years or so.

That last one is a favorite of mine. It reminds me of an old boss I once had who would ask for the impossible on a ridiculous deadline. He would say if I wanted it tomorrow, I'd ask for it tomorrow!

Do you think that the business selling fairy is going to fly down, sprinkle some magic dust on your business and poof, all of the challenges you already know about will just magically fix themselves?

Selling a business has some similarities to selling a house. You probably wouldn't call a realtor and put your house on the market without preparing it to sell, would you? Of course not, unless you're just willing to take the lowball offer because you want to dump it at any cost!

Several years ago, my wife and I thought about upgrading in the town where we live. We invited a good friend, who happens to be a realtor, over to give us his thoughts. He was very clear about the things that needed to be updated in order to get the best offers. We lived in the house for about fifteen years and had done virtually nothing to it. It was new when we bought it, but of course over fifteen years, the styles had changed, and there were plenty of new homes available near us, so there was lots of competition.

Our friend gave us a list of updates: new carpet, kitchen counters, paint, etc. It would have cost about $35,000 to do everything on the list. We probably would have broken even on those investments, but the theory was that the updates would have helped us sell the home faster. In the end, we decided to invest more and make our current house the home of our dreams, and we haven't looked back.

The message from our realtor is the same as my message to business owners. Unless you're willing to dump it for a low price, you need to take the time to prepare it for sale. You need to Plan to Succeed!

Of course, if you have never taken the time to plan an exit strategy, you will have one by default. You'll die behind your desk and the federal government will help you distribute your assets. Sounds great, huh? Not!

You might as well consider the alternatives to actually planning your transition on your terms. It may not be death behind your desk. Statistically speaking, the more likely outcome will be a serious disability that will take you away from your business for an extended amount of time. What happens then? Do you have a strategy in place to keep the business moving forward? Have you discussed your strategy with your employees and family? Do they know your desires and wishes? Will they carry them out?

As previously discussed, a great exit strategy is nothing more than a great business strategy. It's going to tie together the three legs of the stool that Chris Snider outlined—your business goals, your personal goals and your financial goals. If all three are not considered equally, the stool will be wobbly, and you run the risk of toppling over in a bad exit.

Take steps today. Ask the right questions to the right people. Let the right people ask you questions. They are not being judgy or nosey. Just like your doctor, they need to know the facts so they can prescribe the right medicine. They just need to know the truth, so they can help you formulate a strategy. So, who are those right people?

Read on.

TOM BRONSON

CHAPTER 10
BUILD A MOAT OF LEADERS

"I don't want a business that's easy for competitors. I want a business with a moat around it with a very valuable castle in the middle."

–Warren Buffett

Business Magnate, Investor and Philanthropist

When I was in college and the following years, I played lots of tennis, almost every day. I loved the game, even though I was never good enough to play on a team. One pearl of wisdom on leadership I learned from playing tennis is that you don't get better at tennis by playing people worse than you. You can only improve your game by playing with someone better than you. Iron sharpens iron.

The same is true with business allies. You can't get better if you surround yourself with mediocrity. I wish more business owners understood that concept. Unfortunately, some business owners are a mirror to my younger self, full of piss and vinegar. I always knew better than anyone else. It was hard to teach me a lesson, because I knew everything. If only I was as smart as I thought I was.

It's taken me years to learn that I don't know everything. The older I get the dumber I get. Not really, of course, just a self-realization that there is so much I just don't know. I have an insatiable appetite to learn new things! If you catch me watching television, it is most likely programming from the History or Science channels.

What I am suggesting here is that if you're successful, invariably your company will grow beyond your comfort and knowledge. Too often, companies grow to a certain level then stagnate for years, even decades. It does not make them bad companies at all. But it is more difficult to plan and execute a solid exit strategy for a company that has been stale, flat and not grown or innovated in years.

To design and execute a great exit or transition strategy, you need to surround yourself with people who know more about their subject of expertise than you do. The right people will push you beyond your comfort zone.

Over the years, in the various companies I served as the chief executive, I've told a humorous anecdote to prove my point of surrounding myself with great people. More than once on stage or in a magazine article, in response to a question regarding the secrets to my success, I would say, "Surround yourself with great people! Every morning I get out of bed and quickly realize that I'm the dumbest guy in the room!"

If I can't agree with that statement, I've hired the wrong people and need to make a change. Interestingly though, that statement is a bit of an oxymoron. Surrounding myself with the people smarter than I am actually makes me the smartest guy in the room.

Recently I did an interview, and one of the questions I was asked (and is rapidly becoming one of my favorite questions, by the way) is "If you had a superpower, what would it be?" It didn't take me a nanosecond to respond to that one. I do, actually, have a superpower. It's the ability to attract and retain people smarter than I am. They help me grow as a leader and as a company. This strategy hasn't always worked out, but in nearly every case, it's made us a better company and me a better person.

That tactic applied to my last business as much as it applies to my current business. Even as I write this book, I am in awe of the MP team I've been able to recruit, but more on that later.

As a business owner, how much time do you spend thinking about the quality of your team? Are they rock stars, or are they merely adequate? Are they actively taking your business to the next level, or are they happy with the status quo?

I was never a baseball fan growing up. The game seemed slow and boring to me. My wife, on the other hand, has always loved baseball. For the first twenty years of our marriage, every year, in the fall, she would tell me the World Series was on. My response was "Who cares?"

Then, in 2010, the Texas Rangers got hot. Since we live in the Dallas/Fort Worth area, we started to go to a few games, and then suddenly I got it. Baseball fever. I began to understand the strategy and the nuances of the game. I really enjoyed going to the ballpark and watching live. Mind you, I was not a fair-weather friend, the kind that only loves the team when they are doing well. I honestly never watched the game until the Rangers hooked me. That year, the Rangers went on to the World Series and lost against San Francisco, but I got to go to a World Series game.

The Rangers minor league farm team was arguably the best in baseball. The following season, when it became apparent that the Rangers were going to make another run at the title, the general manager knew the team needed more star players. Therefore, he traded away the valuable farm team to load up the roster with new talent. While they made it to the Series again, unfortunately for Ranger fans, they lost to St. Louis. Also, unfortunately for fans, the Rangers no longer had a farm team. We had "bet the farm" for one season.

Rangers fans will debate the wisdom of that decision for decades, but no one doubts that getting the very best players on the team got them to the World Series that year. Like Jack Welch says, be number one or number two or get out of the business. I wish that strategy worked in baseball. There are no prizes for the number two spot.

Find the Best Talent

When you think about surrounding yourself with the best possible team, you have to think of it from two different angles: your internal team and your external team. You have to have a great team inside your organization to carry out your mission. You should surround yourself with a great team of external advisors to carry out any number of missions, including developing a solid transition plan. Let's talk about each of these distinct teams.

Your Internal Team

When I say to hire really great people, I mean take the approach "slow to hire and quick to fire." I always thought Tom Peters coined that term, but a quick internet search got me a number of sources, so who knows. I am confident that Peters' advice is never to hire a person who is missing even a nanosecond on their resume.

The point I'm trying to drive home is to really vet your candidates and never settle for someone if he isn't a perfect fit for your position. Settling leads to discontent, which leads to challenges and issues, which invariably leads to a bad end.

Whenever I've found myself in the unpleasant position of having to let someone go, I always take it very personally. I have failed him by either hiring the wrong person, or by hiring the right person and not providing the tools to make him successful. I realize that sometimes I shouldn't feel that way, but it's my nature. Instinctively, I understand that by severing the relationship, I am doing us both a favor in the long run, but it's still unpleasant, at best. So, set out to find the right people for the right job every time.

And when you hire really great people, you should always share your vision with them. And that vision should be to drive massive value, whatever business you are in. The right people will build the strongest castle. By adding massive value you'll have options for the future, and so will they.

Many owners are afraid that their employees will find out that they are going to sell the business someday. This fear is almost counterintuitive. Every business owner gets into business to someday be able to monetize that asset through an intergenerational transfer, a management transition, or even a sale to a third party. Everyone who has ever gone to work for an entrepreneur instinctively knows that the owner will eventually exit the business. We do have an expiration date, you know.

How can you best share with your team your ultimate goal of exiting the business? Frankly, the express interest in exiting shouldn't be the shared goal. The shared goal should be to build massive value in the business. And if that is your intent, sharing that with your team will ultimately make you a stronger company; you'll attract the best talent, and when the time is right, the transition strategy will present itself.

What I'm suggesting here is to embark on a process to build value. You may be unsure, as most of our clients are, of when and what your exit will look like. But by building massive value in the business, you'll have so many more options available to you when the time is right.

Your External Team

When your goal is to build massive value, not only do you need a solid internal team of employees, it's also very likely that you'll need a solid external team of advisors. I classify external teams into two categories: a value acceleration team and a transaction team. Both are key parts of the moat.

A value acceleration team can take many forms. They are your external advisors, partnered with your internal employees, who help you grow the business and add value.

They can be sales consultants, operational consultants, process engineers, your CPA, or any other external advisor who helps you solve challenges in your business. The very best value acceleration teams have many of these disciplines under one roof. By engaging with a consulting firm that offers these services to you, you can dramatically reduce conflicting advice, and avoid massive internal strife and procrastination when you don't know whose advice to take.

One way to guarantee that you won't have conflicting advice is to select a team which is led by a CEPA. As noted previously, CEPAs have the ability to identify and recruit the type of external talent that works together as a cohesive unit.

These advisors will also tie your value acceleration efforts to a solid transaction team, which is what you'll need to carry out your ultimate goal of exiting the business on your terms.

Like a value acceleration team, a transaction team has many facets. Depending on your ultimate goals, that team would include any number of the following components:

- A Certified Exit Planning Advisor (CEPA)
- A Certified Public Accountant (CPA)
- A Certified Financial Planner (CFP)

- Two different attorneys: an estate planning attorney and a transaction attorney
- A value building team (the same one discussed earlier)
- When appropriate, a family advisor or counselor

Many business owners confuse having a good CPA or attorney with having the right CPA or attorney on a transaction team. It's all too common to have an external CPA who is reactionary, rather than someone who acts as a business advisor. That is not to say that your CPA is wrong, because I know many CPAs who genuinely advise their clients.

Unfortunately, there are also plenty who just do the books or taxes, and that's the extent of their involvement in the business. A great CPA understands that he is an extension of your internal accounting team, and when appropriate, he acts like a CFO for your business when there is not an actual CFO on the team.

The same point applies to attorneys. Most attorneys are specialists in some area of the law: business law, estate planning, litigation, real estate law, employment law. Whatever. It's rare to find one who specializes in a variety of these areas. In fact, the best attorneys know their limitations and regularly make referrals to other attorneys who would best serve their clients.

Some attorneys think making those referrals is a sign of weakness. I would posit that attorneys who don't know all of the answers are the best attorneys, and they make the best business advisors acting as an external general counsel (GC) to their clients. When an owner is large enough to have a GC, he probably handles either business and contract law or litigation and can refer to external resources for all the other disciplines.

Your Leadership Ecosystem

In the end, your leadership ecosystem should consist of a group of internal and external teams of interconnected disciplines. It should be formed by the interaction of a collaborative, like-minded community of professionals with a common goal of building massive value.

Your teams play a major role in your ability to achieve a successful exit. You need strong internal and external teams. Build your moat and surround yourself with the best. And remember, make sure you are the dumbest guy in the room.

For more about the elements you need to build a great internal and external team, download the free e-book, *Assembling the Ultimate Transition Team* from www.MasteryPartners.com.

CHAPTER 11
IDENTIFY RISKS

"Avoiding risk is the riskiest thing you can do in life."

—Unknown

In *The E-Myth* and *The E-Myth Revisited*, author and small business guru Michael Gerber states that 80 percent of new businesses fail in the first five years, and that 80 percent of those remaining will fail in their first ten years. Stated another way, 96 percent of all businesses fail in the first ten years. So, by definition, starting a business is risky. If you're reading this book, there's a good chance that you're a business owner, and therefore, it stands to reason that you are a risk taker.

Somewhere along the path, you made the decision to start or buy a business. Perhaps you weighed all of the positives and negatives by taking a sheet of paper with a line down the middle listing the pros on one side and the cons on the other. Perhaps you were forced into a quick decision because you suddenly found yourself unemployed. Perhaps you thought about it for twenty years and finally pulled the trigger. Regardless, you somehow took that leap and became a business owner. Congratulations.

Feasibly you've made it through the riskiest first five years and way beyond, or maybe you're only a few years into it. Either way, it's likely that many of the benefits of business ownership that were on the positive side of your initial thought process have come to pass. Hopefully your business is providing the lifestyle of which you've dreamed. If it is, chances are pretty good that many of those initial risk factors have lessened or maybe even disappeared by now. Your business is no longer in danger, right? Not so fast.

Sure, the risks have changed, but I posit that there are new risks that have taken their place. Some of the new risks may keep you up at night. It's likely that many of these new risks are out of sight, out of mind for you. So, let's talk about some of the risks of owning a business.

I would classify a business owner's risk into two broad categories: personal and business. Of course, there are items that should appear in both categories, such as debt. These risks are interconnected, where a risk in one category impacts risks in the other. We can't consider just business risks, because it's likely that you and your business are dependent on one another. The business likely needs you to keep the engine humming, and you likely need the business to provide for you and your family.

Earlier we discussed the five D's—death, disability, divorce, distress and disagreement—but there are many more disasters. In his book *Walking to Destiny*, Chris Snider shows just some of the risks you face personally and in your business. This chart illustrates his findings.

PERSONAL	BUSINESS
Accidents	Compliance
Death	Customers
Debt	Data / Information
Disability	Debt
Diversification	Disagreement
Divorce	Distress
Doubt	Economy
Economy	Environment
Fear	Intellectual Property
Health	Interruption
Long Term Care	Key People
Loss of Earning Power	Legal
Taxes	Owner Dependence
Tragedies	Security
	Systems / Processes
	Technology / Machinery

Of course, there are other risks you face personally and in your business, and each one of these items can be broken down into further risks. They are also intertwined. For example, if your business is dependent on you and suddenly tragedy strikes, would the business survive and who would provide for your family?

If your business has a high customer concentration, or is dependent on one customer and that customer leaves or goes out of business, would you suffer a significant loss of income? If a natural disaster occurs and your building is seriously damaged or destroyed, do you have a contingency plan in place to ensure continued operations? Increasingly there is a risk of data being stolen or held hostage. If that theft happens to you, are you prepared? If you are in a partnership or have shareholders and there are differences that become irreconcilable, what happens to the business and to your income? If the economy takes a dive, will it impact your business as well as your other investments? I could go on and on.

The point is, all of these risks can be addressed and either completely eliminated or significantly reduced. Insurance can solve some. Contingency plans can reduce others. Solid plans, processes, training, and systems can handle still others. However, most business owners simply do not prepare for these risks which become roadblocks to growth or transition planning. If they are not addressed long before you decide to transition your business, they can become obstacles that may prevent you from transitioning on your own terms.

If your plan is to sell your business to a third party, or even to your family or management team, the business risks will be uncovered and dissected during due diligence. The buyer could terminate the transaction or require you to take additional risks in the form of contingent consideration, such as owner financing or earn outs. At the very least, the buyer will likely require specific indemnities from you for potential liabilities or expenses.

Knowing that there are significant risks that probably need to be addressed, why don't more business owners do so? Chances are, you probably know many of the risks in your business now, and either feel trapped by them or choose to delay action until you have time to deal with them later. Chances are high that there are risks in your business that you've never even thought about, and you could benefit from a fresh pair of eyes to help identify them. Many owners don't even know the available options for handling specific risks, and that's when a good set of advisors really comes in handy.

When faced with a risk there are only four options for dealing with it: accept, avoid, transfer or reduce.

You can accept the risk and move on. I have identified risks in my businesses that, after weighing the options, I determined I was willing to accept and potentially deal with later. In my case, the cost of the solution was greater than the potential cost of the risk involved, so that decision was easy.

You can avoid dealing with the risk altogether, choosing instead to bury your head in the sand and hope for the best.

If you do that, chances are you will transfer that risk to someone else: your employees, a future buyer, or worse, your family. If you choose to avoid a risk and a tragedy strikes, your family will be left to deal with it, likely triggering other risk factors for them. By the way, here's a side note regarding tragedy. If something does happen, do your employees and family know your desires for how to deal with the issue and beyond? You cannot assume that the situation will be handled the way you desire if you haven't clearly articulated your wishes in advance. There are ways to mitigate this risk as well.

Finally, it's wise to spend time thinking about and identifying your risks so you can work through them and either reduce or eliminate them altogether. Addressing and resolving risks early will ensure that they will not prevent you from transitioning on your terms.

If you'd like to learn more about the hidden risks that may be in your blindspot, download the free e-book *The Blind Spot: Hidden Risks - What You Don't Know Can Hurt You*, from the Downloads tab at www.MasteryPartners.com.

TOM BRONSON

CHAPTER 12
EXECUTE RELENTLESSLY

"Having a vision for what you want is not enough. Vision without execution is hallucination."

–Thomas A. Edison

Inventor and Businessman

A culture of relentless execution is the single most important thing to ensure that you and your business stay on track to meet your ultimate transition goals, regardless of what type of transition you plan to achieve. Without that business mindset, the road forward goes nowhere. So, what does a culture of relentless execution look like?

- The leadership is a team of "you don't have to tell me twice" people who accomplish over 85 percent of the things they set out to achieve.
- The front-line folks just get the job done. After all, they are the most important ones in the company, because they interface with your customers all day long.

- You don't shy away from real challenges, even changing business models or processes, to achieve your goals.
- You hold accountability meetings at least monthly to make sure everyone is on track.
- You hold monthly one-on-ones with your key people to make sure they have the resources needed to get the job done.
- You set quarterly BHAGs (big hairy audacious goals) and achieve them regularly.
- When you miss a target, you regroup, set a new course, and get after it.
- You don't micromanage the team, but you also don't give them a pass when they miss a target.

Is this what your company culture looks like? If not, it's time for a change. To begin to build that culture, start with an honest self-assessment about how your culture compares to one of relentless execution. Where is your company falling short? Do you set targets to achieve the things that will bring more value to your business? Do you intensely hold your people accountable to reaching those targets, and then set new ones? I can tell you that I've been guilty of backsliding in the past. Relentless execution is hard work. If your business approach doesn't look like that, you'll need to make some changes, but you don't have to do it alone. There is help available to you.

To some, this seems like a harsh, almost draconian regimen, especially if your culture looks nothing like that. But having worked in and managed teams like this at various times throughout my career, my experience has been that these are the teams that every professional wants. In addition to handling the day-to-day stuff that their jobs require, they are can-do people that love to achieve more, and the rewards just seem to flow in.

Have you ever been met with a change in the market so abrupt that it left you thinking "How are we going to survive this?" Early in my career, soon after I landed my first management role, our team was served notice in January (on my birthday) by our largest customer that they were leaving us for a competitor. In just ninety days, we were going to lose 30 percent of our business. 30 percent! Having just been named sales manager, I thought this was going to be a short career!

But, I pulled the team together and told them we had a choice. We could either accept the news and plan to dramatically cut the operation to the new normal, or we could figure out how to gain all that business back! Every person in the company pitched in, from sales to operations to service. No opportunity was left untouched. By December 31st, we had not only recovered all of the lost business, we had actually grown 5 percent. Everyone in the company was euphoric. We had set the stage for massive growth over the next five years. And, the challenge solved our customer concentration risk long before I even knew what that was.

When something like challenge that happens in your business, and invariably it does in every business, which team would you rather have on your side? The one that accepts the blow or the relentless execution one? I can answer that question for you.

If your team is not already a relentless execution team, shifting cultures will be difficult at first, and you'll want to give it up at the first sign of trouble. There will be conscientious objectors on the team. You will either have to win them over or make a change. If your senior team doesn't get behind this new mindset, you'll be fighting an uphill battle.

When you do get them moving in the right direction, momentum will take over, and you'll achieve more and more until you forget what it looked like in the past. Your team will start to love the new culture, and even better, the front-line folks will get behind it. Now you've got an engine that can handle whatever gets thrown at it.

Set Goals

Setting goals is a key part of execution. You've likely heard of SMART goals, a concept first introduced by George Doran in 1981 and modified over time, and there is a good chance you have used them in the past or use them today.

<u>S</u>pecific: State exactly what you'll do.

<u>M</u>easurable: Be able to evaluate the results.

<u>A</u>chievable: Make it attainable.

<u>R</u>elevant: Make it pertinent.

<u>T</u>ime-bound: Set a specific date to achieve the outcome.

Exit Planning Institute CEO Chris Snider uses SMART goals to achieve results with his clients. But his SMART Goals have a little twist. Chris replaces <u>A</u>chievable with <u>A</u>spirational. It's a nuance for sure, but it really makes a difference. Everyone can set goals that are achievable. In a culture of relentless execution, that's just not enough. Goals are meant to stretch you. It's important to reach for meaningful goals. By substituting Aspirational for Achievable, you move the target just out of reach to make the team stretch just a bit. This target is not so lofty that you miss each one, but just above the comfort zone, so you reach the target and stretch the team. Here are Chris's SMART goals:

Specific: State exactly what you'll do.

Measurable: Be able to evaluate the results.

Aspirational: Stretch beyond your comfort zone.

Relevant: Make it pertinent.

Time-bound: Set a specific date to achieve the outcome.

Do you write down your goals? I always write my goals on paper and put them in my path. I find that if I don't write them down, I run the risk of forgetting about them, or worse, letting myself off the hook when I don't achieve the result. I need written goals to hold myself accountable. Believe me, there are plenty of distractions to keep me off course. If your goals don't meet the new SMART definition, then rewrite them now to make sure they do.

Using SMART goals is a very easy way to start, and the process requires little training. Just follow the rules written right into the acronym. If you want a more advanced course in achieving goals, I strongly recommend you read *TRACTION* by Gino Wickman. *TRACTION* is the basis for the Entrepreneurial Operating System (EOS). The processes for setting and achieving goals using EOS are brilliant and pretty simple to follow. There are lots of free tools available at the EOS Worldwide website. If you're up for a more complete method to get your team involved, I highly recommend it.

Manage Distractions

Distractions are those fun little things that seem to knock you off course regularly. In most cases, distractions keep you from achieving your dreams and goals. They have a way of making you feel productive, but they actually stand between you and greatness.

Distractions are the daily fires that will never go away. Distractions always seem more important than exit planning. I mean, after all, I'm not really going to sell this business for several years. I'll get back to planning later. Famous last words.

My father was one of my greatest mentors and told me a parable about the power of distractions:

A construction worker who worked on high-rise buildings would leave the work site every day for twenty years with a wheelbarrow full of dirt. Every day, the security guards would stop him and search the dirt because they were certain that he was stealing something, but they never found anything in the dirt. Finally, after years of this madness it was time for him to retire. On his last day as he walked through the gate one last time with his wheelbarrow full of dirt, the guards just couldn't stand it any longer. "We give up," they said. "We know you've been stealing something all these years, but we can't figure it out. It's killing us, so since this is your last day, we promise not to press charges if you just tell us what it was so we can satisfy our curiosity." The worker smiled and simply said, "wheelbarrows."

How do you manage your distractions? Are you like most business owners who arrive at the office early to get some work done, and then your team arrives, and the relentless interruptions ensue? Before you know it, it's the end of their day, and you find that you're still doing the very thing you were doing when your team arrived that morning. Sure, some of the interruptions may be necessary, but for the most part, they keep you from focusing on what's important. I can't say enough about managing your own time and providing an environment that allows your team to do the same. If you're constantly interrupting your people, they probably feel the same way you do about distractions.

So you've set the goal of building massive value in your business, and yet you allow yourself to indulge in these unnecessary distractions. There must be a better way.

I finally solved the crisis of distractions by setting up weekly 30-minute, one-on-one meetings with my direct reports. The agenda was simple. First, we covered their list, then mine. Usually there was plenty of time to catch up on family and personal stuff. My instruction to them was that if something came up that was important and urgent, bring it right away, but if it could wait, add it to your list, and we would cover it in our one-on-one.

I piled all of my one-on-ones in one day, back to back. It was grueling at first, but then I realized how much time I gained by virtually eliminating the daily distractions. The most important outcome was that by having more time available to me, I used some of that time to just think and stretch my entrepreneurial legs.

The strategy was so effective, we implemented it throughout the entire organization. The system was crude but effective. In retrospect, I wish I'd discovered *TRACTION* before I started it, because the EOS system is so much better. Its tools for operating a business streamline every process.

Embrace the Power of Deadlines

I have been accused of being a closet procrastinator for my whole life. Frankly, and to be perfectly honest, I am. I think it's just human nature. I actually used to thrive on dealing with all of the distractions that came my way, so much so, that I had to use techniques to keep focused.

One of my favorite books is *Focus* by Al Ries, founder of consulting firm Ries & Ries. In it he says that "Good things happen when you narrow your focus." He's right. I find that nothing narrows my focus better than deadlines. I love deadlines. Deadlines mean that a project has an expiration date. When I set deadlines, I never miss them. Conversely, if I have a hard time setting a deadline on a project, it's probably because it's not important enough to get done, which should be my signal to toss it in the trash.

Finally—

What do goal setting, distractions and deadlines have to do with exit planning? Well, everything. It goes back to building value.

First, when you start preparing your business for transition, at least three to five years before you actually want to transition, there are going to be things in your business that need to be addressed. Hard things. If you have a relentless execution team, you'll be able to make the changes you need to build massive additional value to your business. And, if you want to sell your business to an outside individual or firm, buyers tend to pay more for teams that get the job done. Smart buyers will examine every nuance of your team dynamics. They clearly understand that they are not just buying your customer list or your product. They are investing in your people.

If you are not operating at this level already, this kind of culture shift will take time. Which is why there is no time to waste, especially if you are planning to exit your business in the next three to five years.

CHAPTER 13
UNDERSTAND THE PROCESS

"No matter how great the talent or efforts, some things just take time. You can't produce a baby in one month by getting nine women pregnant."

–Warren Buffett

Business Magnate, Investor and Philanthropist

"Are we there yet?"

–Every child who has ever been on a long car trip

As we've already discussed, exit strategies fail four out of five times. One of the major causes of these epidemic failures is that many business owners think that selling a business is like selling a house. You call a real estate agent, do a few things, list the house on the market, and poof, you're moving into a new place in typically three to six months. (Although I once had a house that sat on the market for over a year, and I once sold a house myself in six hours before it was ever listed, but these are stories for another time.)

Selling a business is not like that. Selling a house is more like a sprint, and selling a business is more like a marathon. There are far fewer agents to list the business, and there is precious little in terms of comparables, or comps. In housing, you can get literally hundreds of comps and stats for every house sold or even listed. You can find out the square footage, how many days on the market, number of bedrooms and bathrooms. The MLS is literally a profusion of information waiting to be mined.

There is no MLS for businesses. Most private transactions are never listed anywhere. No listing. No comps. No number of days on the market. No figures on profitability. Nothing.

You're left to draw your own conclusions from the tiny bit of available data. You can review information widely published about either large company acquisitions or small startups who sold to a giant strategic buyer for a billion dollars. And, you can glean information from your friends at a dinner party over a nice bottle of wine. These are the outliers. Most of the hearsay is just false narrative.

The fact is, selling a business takes time. Many deals fall apart because of seller fatigue. Sellers get tired of the process taking so long. Sellers get frustrated with the seemingly endless barrage of due diligence questions. Sellers get angry with offers that are way below what the business is worth. Sellers get tired of having to gather data that's just not available in their systems. Sellers get frustrated that buyers just don't get how good this business is today. Sellers explode when the deal is invariably "retraded," a term we use for lowering the price at the last minute. By the way, most buyers do this, so you need to be prepared.

Those buyers, on the other hand, want to dive as deep as they can in the pool. They want to search through every nook and cranny. They want to look at things of which you've probably never even thought. Every time they see something that seems out of whack, the distraction causes them to wonder what else they are missing, so they dig deeper.

Make no mistake. Due diligence is a necessary part of any sale process. The seller needs to understand what the buyers want. Like a home inspection that is designed to either get you to do things the buyers want or lower the price before they close the transaction, due diligence is the same. Many buyers dig as deep as they can to find ways to lower the price.

By the way, when you get that initial offer, say a range of $5 to $6 million, or $25 to $32 million, sellers only see the top number. They will be able to negotiate a little higher during the process. Buyers only see the bottom number and believe that is the starting point for lowering the price. The best advice we give our clients is to forget the top number. Recognize that in most cases, this particular buyer believes the bottom number is the maximum they will pay, and they will do their very best to reduce it from there.

Let's get back to the house sale analogy. If you've ever listed a home for sale, you probably called a real estate agent whom you trust to come in and give an evaluation. Good ones, and there are plenty, will tell you what buyers want. They will be armed with stats and trends in home sales that will help you get the best price for your home. They will also tell you that with a little work, you can probably get a better price.

For example, new carpet and paint are important. If your kitchen is dated, a reasonable investment there will probably give you a decent return. If you add a pool, a good realtor will tell you that's a bad investment. In our area, a pool will increase the value of the home by about $10,000, a terrible return for a pool that cost you $60,000 to put in. So, your realtor will give you a list of items to fix, and then you'll balance the work against the return and determine what needs to get done before you list the house. Once it's listed, it has to stay immaculate. No small chore if you have children.

So, what does it look like when you sell your business? Depending on your size, you'll either call a business broker or an investment banker. I know "banker" is a strange name for someone who is not loaning you money. I didn't make the rules. For the purpose of this discussion, I'll just use the term broker for either of these. You call in your broker, who just like a real estate agent, doesn't get paid until a sale is closed. His primary objective is to get you listed as quickly as possible, regardless of the condition of the business. He won't see a payday unless he gets you across the finish line. Think of it as a success fee.

This situation is the equivalent of a real estate agent listing your house before you've even vacuumed the floors. In my opinion, this is another reason that the process takes so much time, and why four out of five businesses never close a transaction. Don't get me wrong, a broker will do his level best to sell your business in its current condition. He will probably give you a list of stuff that you should prepare, but he is not typically all that concerned about the current state of affairs. The broker is an expert in positioning the current state in as good a light as possible. If you put lipstick on a pig, it might be a little cuter, but it's still a pig.

According to Zillow in 2018, the average home took sixty-eight days from listing to close. This stat comes from solid data. As we've already said, there is very little data available on business transactions. A fun little game I played while writing this was to Google "How long does it take to sell a business." I took the data from the top search results, a wide variety of websites including business brokers, investment bankers, and even the Small Business Administration, and put it in a spreadsheet. The average of this completely unscientific process was twelve months, with a range of three months to two years. The average is about 5 1/2 times the length of time to sell a house. So, let's just say it takes a lot longer.

I'm not telling you all this to get you depressed, although it depresses me to think about it. I'm telling you this because there is a better way.

My company is a virtual pioneer in the presale value acceleration market. Although we aren't the first to grasp this concept, we are one of the first to bring all of the disciplines under one roof. Mastery does not even accept clients that have less than a two- to three-year transition horizon. Our mission is to provide an honest opinion regarding the current state of the business, including transaction readiness and valuation. We then help our clients truly define their desired outcome and provide them a roadmap to get there.

Sometimes that roadmap is challenging, and our clients engage with us to help them improve the value of their precious asset. Other times, the road seems fairly straight forward, and our clients choose to do it themselves, sort of a DIY approach. For those clients who engage with us, we have all of the necessary expertise available inside our value acceleration team, from finance to sales, from process to legal, from branding to... well you get the picture. All of that expertise is available to our clients as needed.

While the company is being prepared properly, we bring in our transition team of experts to talk about things like estate and tax planning, financial planning, family issues, and legal preparation.

Our passion is fixing a broken system. It makes me angry that 83 percent of companies that come on the market each year never close a transaction. We're out to fix that, one company at a time. Because I've done one hundred transactions myself, as either buyer or seller, I always wondered why this type of service was not available in the market. We're virtually pioneers in this space.

It bears repeating, the best transitions teams have at least one CEPA involved, and the very best have multiple CEPAs across many disciplines on the team. Of the 1,000+ CEPAs, only about 10 percent of them are experts in value acceleration. It's really important to have at least one value accelerator on your transition team.

At Mastery, our value acceleration team rigorously follows a process that closely mirrors the CEPA value acceleration process. Whether you're working with Mastery or some other trained professionals in the art and science of improving company value, it will take time to make those improvements and realize the results. In businesses, you can't just make quick changes that will improve the outcome. There are some cosmetic changes that will help, but to really move the needle on the outcome, the changes will take time to produce results.

Most buyers will look at Trailing Twelve Months (TTM) of performance. If you make a change to profitability and see the results in the first quarter, a buyer will question the result until you have a track record of sustainability. And if your financial improvement is sustainable, you need to give it time to improve the long-term value of the business.

For example, let's say that your business makes $100,000 a month in EBITDA, and you make some improvements that double the profitability. Easier said than done, but I've seen it more often than you think! Let's also assume that your industry trades at an average of 3X EBITDA.

(In Thousands)	BASELINE YEAR 1				YEAR 2			
	Q1	Q2	Q3	Q4	Q1	Q2	Q3	Q4
EBITDA	300	300	300	300	600	600	600	600
TTM	1,200	1,200	1,200	1,200	1,500	1,800	2,100	2,400
Multiple	3	3	3	3	3	3	3	3
Value Estimate	3,600	3,600	3,600	3,600	4,500	5,400	6,300	7,200

The example above is a simplistic visualization of what happens to the valuation over the TTM. As you can see, the profitability doubled right away, and the value moved up significantly— almost $1M. But it takes a full year to realize the value for those changes that were made immediately, changes that effectively double the valuation of the business.

Most changes you make will not find their way to your financials immediately. They will take much longer to realize. Of course, profitability is only one item that will impact the overall value, but this example shows why it takes time to even prepare a business for sale, much less sell it.

When preparing a business for transition, the process is important. It's important to follow a strict regimen that will add massive value long term. Then you can realize the full potential no matter what your transition looks like and hunker down for the long haul.

ACT THREE

SO NOW WHAT?

CHAPTER 14
THE THIRD ACT

"Life is a moderately good play with a badly written third act."

—Truman Capote

Novelist, Playwright and Actor

Remember when you were a kid and people would ask you what you wanted to be when you grow up? It was fun to daydream about all of the possibilities! I was going to be someone famous! I wanted to be an actor or maybe a musician or maybe a corporate big shot who everyone knows and loves. To be perfectly honest, author never crossed my five-year-old mind for sure! A close friend always wanted to be a sanitation worker, you know, a garbage man. That was honestly his dream purely because he wanted to ride on the back of the truck the way they do when they ride around your neighborhood. We still laugh about that.

It didn't matter what you wanted to do. It was always fun to daydream about it!

When was the last time you did that? Yes, go ahead and daydream about what you want to be when you grow up!

And don't dismiss that as a silly waste of time and try to skip this chapter. I want you to really think for a bit about what you want to do once you transition your business.

I've already told you how many businesses come on the market that just don't sell—83 percent! Let's talk a bit more about the 17 percent that do actually close a transaction.

Of the group that succeeds in closing a transaction, only 40 percent are satisfied with the transition and their own lives a year later. There are lots of reasons for this situation, but the most prevalent is that the owners are not prepared for what we call "Act Three." Act One, youth, seemed to fly by. We spent the bulk of our lives in Act Two, our career(s). With life expectancy continuing to rise, we're increasingly spending more time in Act Three, enjoying the spoils of our hard work.

What does Act Three look like for you? What will be your purpose? Are you going to volunteer? Start another business venture? Travel the world? Tick items off your bucket list? Play golf?

Do you openly talk about Act Three with your family? Are your family members involved in the business? Is your exit strategy to transition the business to them? And are you going to be able to step out of the way and let the next generation actually run the business, or are you going to be all up in their business all of the time? By the way, family or intergenerational transitions are barely more successful than selling the business outright, with only a 30 percent success rate in moving to the second generation. The odds diminish with each successive generation.

Things can get messy and confusing quickly, especially if you don't have a plan for Act Three. You should rehearse for Act Three. Give it a test drive. Stay out of the business one day a week to go volunteer, or play golf, or whatever. Take an extended vacation for three or four weeks, and stay disconnected from the office. Don't check emails or voice mails. If you're not used to being disconnected, ease into it. Start by checking messages only every other day, then every three days, then once a week. Can you relax?

Business owners tell me all the time that they are tied to the business 24/7. Even when they are on vacation, they field calls. They are in constant contact; they check emails every time the cell buzzes. "My family doesn't mind. They understand that's just the way it is!" they say. Really? BS. You can't replace undivided attention. It's amazing!

One of my early mentors forced me to decompress. It was one of the greatest gifts he could have ever given me. I took extended vacations from the very beginning of my career and was totally disconnected. I bet you haven't. It was challenging at first. It's more challenging today with all the ways we can connect. I encourage you to give it a try.

So why, you ask, am I so passionate about Act Three and preparing for it?

I've been lucky enough to be surrounded by many great mentors throughout my career. Some would say it's luck. Others would call it a coincidence. I have relentlessly worked to sharpen my saw so I can raise my game. While I have purposely tried to learn from those whom I perceived to be great leaders with lots to offer, I have been lucky enough to have worked with many of them through the years.

One of the greatest mentors I had the pleasure of learning from was my father. He did not have an MBA from an ivy league school. In fact, he had no degree at all. My father always said he got his masters from the "school of hard knocks," and his Ph.D. from "Whatsamatta U." He was a man who understood his own strengths and weaknesses. My father was a technical genius but didn't know how to sell his way out of a wet paper bag. So, he enrolled in a Dale Carnegie course, "How to Win Friends and Influence People," and learned the skills he needed to put food on our table. He taught us to do whatever it takes. That's powerful.

Perhaps the greatest business lessons I learned from my father were not actually business lessons at all, chiefly the work ethic he instilled in me and my siblings. He would say, "Son, I don't care what you do for a living. Be a ditch digger if you want to be. But, if you're a ditch digger, you better dig the biggest, baddest ditches on the planet."

My father taught me the value of money. We didn't have any growing up. Although my mother denied it to her dying day, having Spam for dinner was a real treat for us! So, when I wanted a bike, and it wasn't my birthday or Christmas (my birthday and Christmas are only 16 days apart, which is a conspiracy I won't go into now), he offered to lend me the money for the bike at 10 percent. I was twelve. I still have the bike.

Fast forward a few years. Dad was able to build a very successful business, ultimately employing seventy-five "families," as he called our employees. Although he never wanted us to work in his business, my brother and I found our way there. We had, and still have, very different skill sets. I'm a born salesperson, and he is a natural at operations and finance, although he does sell for a living as of this writing.

Later, when my brother and I took over the business, we had a natural division of duties. We would say that we split the responsibilities right down the middle, fifty-fifty. I would make ridiculous promises, and he would keep them. Now that is relentless execution! And, he was damn good at it. Try as I might, I was never able to make a promise on which he couldn't deliver.

The reason we got to that place was because of the encouragement of our mutual mentor and father. We were in the habit of bringing Dad (we called him Bill in the office) our harebrained ideas for how to grow the business or change our processes or whatever. Dad always gave us the same answer, "Sounds interesting. Why don't you give it a try?" So, we did.

Some of our ideas didn't exactly pan out (that's another book), but others were wildly successful. Some ideas were so successful that we had a compound annual growth rate of nearly 50 percent for five years. That result led us to a successful merger with four similar companies to form a regional powerhouse, and then a successful exit to a large publicly traded buyer. But I'll get back to that.

The lesson of how Dad allowed us to pursue our ridiculous goals escaped me until much later when I asked him about why he did it. He told me that, in fact, he thought that most of our ideas would never amount to much, and that he'd already tried most of them and failed. Dad told me how proud he was when we took ideas he knew wouldn't work, and yet somehow, we accomplished them. In his words, he was astonished at the results, and it made him realize the power of letting people try.

My father taught us to listen to new ideas and try new things. He gave us enough rope to go out and hang ourselves if we failed. He relentlessly supported us. Suddenly it dawned on me that trying new things was the key to success, and I didn't have to have all the great ideas. This freedom has driven me to allow those I've surrounded myself with through the years to try new things that stretch our limits and set new bars. To be sure, not every new idea has worked. In fact, we've had some colossal failures. But we've also had some enormous successes! Those are the ones I choose to dwell on.

So, after building that business, merging with others, and selling ourselves to the large, publicly traded buyer, my father, who I always considered to be lower middle class, was finally set for the rest of his life. He exited with great joy and high expectations, only to be buried three short years later.

You see, my father had battled cancer for twenty-one years. He was a real cancer survivor story. In the end, the cancer was the cause of death on his death certificate. But I submit that it was actually something else that killed Dad. He never thought about or focused on the "what's next" part of selling his business. He had no plan for what to do for his Third Act. He was distraught.

The business was my father's life. The business defined him. The business gave him purpose. After Dad sold it, he no longer had a reason to get out of bed in the morning. He wasted away watching reruns on television. Dad felt he had let his employees down. In reality, they had much greater opportunities in a bigger company, and many of them went on to build extremely successful careers with the buyer. The official cause of death was cancer. But I know what really killed him, a lack of purpose. I vowed that fate would never happen to me, and that I would help others to learn from that lesson, so that it would never happen again on my watch.

That event was twenty years ago this week, as I write this. He was my mentor, and I miss him. But his lessons live on in me and the others he touched.

Have a purpose to your Third Act. You also need to think about setting aside some time to adjust to the new reality. For my father, it was almost a grieving process. The exhilaration of selling, and then the sudden stop with no transition, was like grieving the loss of his creation, something he'd built from nothing. So, even when your intention from the beginning is to sell, be prepared for it.

The end of Act Two does not have to be the end. If properly planned and executed, it can be the beginning of a glorious Act Three.

TOM BRONSON

Acknowledgements

Where do I start for the inspiration for this book?

First, I want to acknowledge the amazing people I've had the opportunity to lead through the years. You have helped me more than you realize. I've used your skills and talents as my training ground to prove, or more frequently disprove, my harebrained theories on leadership and building value. In many cases, you've been the proving ground for my hypotheses on exit strategies.

Second, to my wonderful wife, partner and best friend, Karen, and our three amazing daughters. Your support of my sometimes ridiculous ideas has given me the strength to carry on and see my dreams through to reality, even when I have put us at great financial risk.

Third, to my partners at Mastery. I have lived out my mission of surrounding myself with people who are way smarter than I am. You make me better, and you deliver incredible value to our clients. That partnership extends to Chris Snider and the Exit Planning Institute. While Mastery's processes are its own, the things I learned while training for my CEPA certification helped me to refine our process and are now permanently intertwined with our methodology.

Finally, to the mentors from whom I have had the privilege of learning. You have poked and prodded and tugged me, sometimes against extreme resistance, to learn and grow and refine my style. I promise that every lesson you taught me has shaped me into the leader I've become. You have also helped me make this book a reality. Particularly, Rich Cavaness, who has been a great friend and mentor to help me navigate the writing and publishing process. Nancy Baldwin, who has patiently helped me through the editing process. And Kim Bentson, my sidekick who helped me refine the concepts, remember personal stories, and who really makes me look good—and that's a tall order.

Most importantly, I want to thank the greatest mentor I ever had—my father. Unfortunately, you did not live to see the fruit of your labor in me, but I am comforted by the fact that you are watching over me even now. I love you, Dad. Thanks for never giving up on me.

RECOMMENDED READING LIST

- Reis, Al. *Focus: The Future of Your Company Depends on It.*
  New York: Harper Business, 1996, 2005.

- Koch, Charles G. *Good Profit: How Creating Value for Others Built One of the World's Most Successful Companies.* New York: Crown Business, 2015

- Collins, Jon. *Good to Great: Why Some Companies Make the Leap and Others Don't.*
  New York: Harper Collins, 2001

- Rose, R. Michael. *ROE Powers ROI: The Ultimate Way to Think and Communicate for Ridiculous Results.* Dallas: Brown Books Publishing Group, 2012

- Gerber, Michael E. *The E-Myth Revisited: Why Most Small Businesses Don't Work and What to Do About It.* New York: Harper Collins, 1995, 2001

- Achor, Shawn. *The Happiness Advantage: The Seven Principles of Positive Psychology That Fuel Success and Performance at Work.* New York: Crown Books, 2010

- Covey, Stephen R. *The 7 Habits of Highly Effective People: Powerful Lessons in Personal Change.* New York: Simon & Schuster, 1989, 2004

- Wickman, Gino. *Traction: Get a Grip on Your Business.* Dallas: BenBella Books, 2011

- Snider, Christopher M. *Walking to Destiny: 11 Actions an Owner Must Take to Rapidly Grow Value & Unlock Wealth.* Cleveland: ThinkTank Publishing House, 2016

- And loads more. If you don't already, learn to love to read or get Audible!

ADDITIONAL RESOURCES

Connect with Tom Bronson to discuss how Mastery Partners can help you get on track to successfully transition your business on your terms.

Contact Tom for speaking at your next event!

- Keynote addresses
- Motivational Talks
- "How To" Seminars & Workshops

Topics include—

- Building Value in Your Business
- Business Transitions
- Exit Strategies
- Leadership
- Innovation
- Being a Man of God
- And many customized messages...

e: tom@masterypartners.com

c: 817.797.1488

www.MasteryPartners.com, where there are lots of free tools available on the Tools tab

www.TomBronsonSpeaks.com

About the Author

Tom Bronson is the founder and president of Mastery Partners, LLC. Bronson founded Mastery Partners to help business owners grow and exit their businesses. As a business owner, he has been in your situation one hundred times (literally), and he knows what you don't know, yet. Bronson is passionate about helping people and has the experience to do it.

Mastery's Partners are accomplished executives with a ton of experience from startups to Fortune 500 companies. They are the people you want on your team when you are facing tough business situations. Whether it be exit strategy, transition plans, mergers and acquisitions, sales slumps, operational headaches, people problems, or you name it, these executives have seen it all many times and made it out the other side—with success. Let them help you with a free consultation today.

Mastery is a firm that helps business owners seize opportunities and realize profound economic success through innovative processes and proven expertise. Its Partners specialize in helping small to midsize businesses navigate and execute a solid exit strategy.

Before devoting his work to Mastery Partners full-time, Bronson served as president and CEO of Granbury Solutions. Bronson founded Granbury Solutions in 2010 with the acquisition of five of the hospitality industry's most promising tech companies. Granbury introduced the industry's first recurring revenue model by offering an end-to-end suite of technology for restaurants, including point of sale, online ordering, mobile apps, loyalty, and marketing services.

Under Bronson's leadership, the Granbury Solutions technology offering has expanded to serve the restaurant, craft beverage, wine, bar, and specialty retail markets. Since its founding, Granbury Solutions has enjoyed consistent annual growth and serves more than nine thousand customers worldwide, landing it on the Inc. 5000 list and in the top ten of Tech Titans fastest growing technology companies in North Texas in consecutive years. Bronson was also a finalist for the Ernst & Young EY Entrepreneur of the Year award.

Tom Bronson is a Certified Exit Planning Advisor (CEPA). In addition to being a consultant, he has served as president of Business Navigators, a servant leadership organization that helps businesses through outreach, education, and community service. Bronson is the voice of the Southlake Dragon Marching Band.

He is also a sought-after speaker who frequents many venues sharing his vast knowledge and industry expertise as well as lending his talents to Software Executive Magazine serving on its editorial board.

Made in the USA
Middletown, DE
09 January 2020